Understanding the
Bill of Rights

Sally Senzell Isaacs

Crabtree Publishing Company
www.crabtreebooks.com

Author: Sally Senzell Isaacs
Editor-in-Chief: Lionel Bender
Editor: Kelley MacAulay
Proofreaders: Adrianna Morganelli,
    Crystal Sikkens
Project editor: Robert Walker
Photo research: Susannah Jayes
Designer: Malcolm Smythe
Production coordinator: Katherine Kantor
Production: Kim Richardson
Prepress technician: Margaret Amy Salter
Consultant: Professor Richard Jensen,
    history teacher, consultant, and author

This book was produced for
    Crabtree Publishing Company
    by Bender Richardson White, U.K.

Cover:
Demonstrator at Los Angeles illegal immigrant
rally, May 1, 2006; Dome of the Capitol Building
in Washington D. C.; One of only two copies of
the United States Bill of Rights

Title page:
A trial by jury in the 1800s

Photographs:
© Corbis: Bettmann: p. 26, 28; Bob Krist: p. 20
© Northwind Picture Archives: p. 1, 6, 7,
    9, 10, 11, 13, 14, 15, 16, 18, 19, 22, 25, 29
© Shutterstock.com: cover (Capitol building and
    man), p. 4, 17, 23, 27
© The Granger Collection: p. 8, 12
© Wikipedia.com: cover (background)

Library and Archives Canada Cataloguing in Publication

Isaacs, Sally Senzell, 1950-
    Understanding the Bill of Rights / Sally Senzell Isaacs.

(Documenting early America)
Includes index.
ISBN 978-0-7787-4374-3 (bound).--ISBN 978-0-7787-4379-8 (pbk.)

    1. United States. Constitution. 1st-10th Amendments—Juvenile
literature. 2. Constitutional amendments--United States--Juvenile
literature. 3. Civil rights--United States--Juvenile literature.
I. Title. II. Series: Isaacs, Sally Senzell, 1950- . Documenting
early America.

KF4750.I83 2008   j342.7308'5   C2008-905554-3

Library of Congress Cataloging-in-Publication Data

Isaacs, Sally Senzell, 1950-
    Understanding the Bill of Rights / Sally Senzell Isaacs.
        p. cm. -- (Documenting early America)
    Includes index.

    ISBN-13: 978-0-7787-4379-8 (pbk. : alk. paper)
    ISBN-10: 0-7787-4379-9 (pbk. : alk. paper)
    ISBN-13: 978-0-7787-4374-3 (reinforced library binding : alk. paper)
    ISBN-10: 0-7787-4374-8 (reinforced library binding : alk. paper)

    1. United States. Constitution. 1st-10th Amendments--Juvenile litera-
ture. 2. Constitutional amendments--United States--Juvenile literature. 3.
Civil rights--United States--Juvenile literature. I. Title.

    KF4750.I83 2008
    342.7308'5--dc22
                                                2008036602

Crabtree Publishing Company
www.crabtreebooks.com   1-800-387-7650

Published in Canada
Crabtree Publishing
616 Welland Ave.
St. Catharines, Ontario
L2M 5V6

Published in the United States
Crabtree Publishing
PMB16A
350 Fifth Ave., Suite 3308
New York, NY 10118

Published in the United Kingdom
Crabtree Publishing
White Cross Mills
High Town, Lancaster
LA1 4XS

Published in Australia
Crabtree Publishing
386 Mt. Alexander Rd.
Ascot Vale (Melbourne)
VIC 3032

Contents

The Bill of Rights

The United States **Constitution** is a written plan or set of rules for the national **government**. It explains how laws are made, how leaders are chosen, and what the national government can and cannot do.

The Constitution includes ten **amendments**. An amendment is an addition. These ten amendments are called the **Bill of Rights.** They give the American people important rights and freedoms. The Constitution was approved by the national government in 1788. The Bill of Rights became part of the Constitution three years later, in 1791.

▲ *The United States Constitution*

The Bill of Rights: Ten Amendments

First Freedom of religion, speech, the press, assembly (meeting), and petition (demanding change)

Second The right to bear arms (guns)

Third During peacetime, citizens cannot be forced to feed and house soldiers

Fourth People and homes cannot be searched without a good reason

Fifth People accused of crimes must be treated fairly

Sixth The right to a speedy, public, and fair trial

Seventh The right to a **jury** trial

Eighth Punishment may not be cruel and unusual

Ninth Americans have other rights, even if they are not listed in the Bill of Rights. As questions arise, judges will decide about other rights

Tenth The U.S. government has only the powers listed in the Constitution

A new way forward

The Bill of Rights was created at a time when the United States had only recently been formed. Before this time, people in America were not always free to say and do as they wished or to follow their religious beliefs. Some people were sent to jail without first having a fair **trial.** The Bill of Rights provided Americans with certain freedoms that can never be taken away.

Dealing with Taxes

Before the United States became a nation, it was 13 **colonies**. A colony is a place where people live that is far from the country that rules it. Britain ruled the 13 colonies for many years. Colonists had to follow Britain's laws and pay **taxes** to Britain. A tax is money that people pay to the government to run a country.

▼ *A map of the 13 American colonies ruled by Britain*

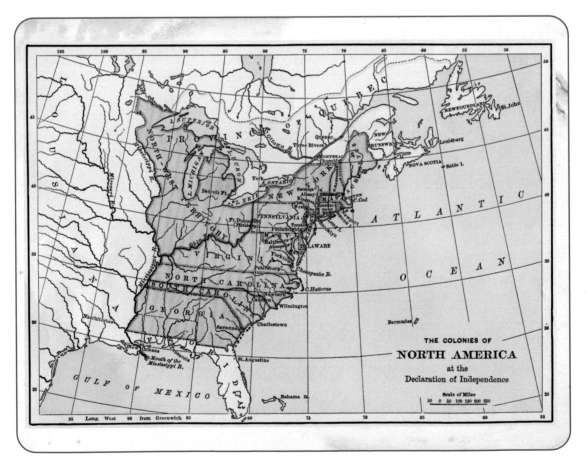

◄ *Colonial leaders met in houses and taverns to make plans for the Congress.*

The first Congress

By 1765, colonists were angry with Britain. Britain's government kept adding new taxes. Every time the colonists bought such items as newspapers, cloth, sugar, or tea, they had to pay extra money to Britain. In 1774, leaders from the colonies decided to work together to solve their issues with Britain. They held a meeting in Philadelphia called the **Continental Congress**. Each colony sent **representatives** to the meeting. A representative is someone who speaks for other people. At the meeting, the representatives discussed their problems with Britain.

Fighting for Freedom

Britain's King George III heard about the Continental Congress. He wondered how the colonists could turn against their country like this! He sent soldiers to the colonies to keep the colonists under control. The king created laws that forced the colonists to let British soldiers live in their houses. Then the king told the colonists to stop having meetings about Britain's rule. The colonists refused to stop and held their meetings secretly.

▲ *People in New York, angry with British laws and taxes, tore down a statue of King George III.*

The Revolution begins

In April 1775, about 700 British soldiers headed to the towns of Lexington and Concord, Massachusetts. They had heard that colonial soldiers there were collecting guns. When the armed colonists met the British soldiers, a battle broke out between them. This was the first battle in the **American Revolution**. A **revolution** is a strong action by people to change their government. The American Revolution lasted for six years. The colonists who fought for independence from Britain were called **Patriots**.

▲ *Paul Revere warned the colonists in Massachusetts*

Messages on horseback
The colonists in Lexington were ready to protect themselves against the British soldiers because they were warned by Paul Revere and William Dawes that soldiers were on their way. The two men rode through the town shouting, *"The British are coming!"*

Independence

While the American and British soldiers were fighting the war, leaders from the colonies continued to meet. They planned the **Declaration of Independence**. This document would announce that the colonies wanted to separate from Britain. The leaders wanted to create their own government and their own laws.

▲ *British soldiers—known as "redcoats" because of their uniforms—fought in many battles against the Patriots in the American Revolution.*

For freedom and rights

Thomas Jefferson wrote the Declaration of Independence. In it he wrote that people are born with rights that a government cannot take away. These rights include the right to life, liberty, and happiness. *Liberty* is another word for "freedom." The Declaration also said that *"all men are created equal."* This means that no one person should have more rights than another.

On July 4, 1776, Congress voted "yes" to accept the Declaration of Independence. In 1781, the Patriots won the American Revolution. The 13 colonies became 13 states and the United States of America was born.

◄ *Thomas Jefferson wrote the Declaration of Independence.*

A New Government

With the Declaration of Independence in mind, Congress began planning a new national government. The leaders of the states agreed to form a national government but they wanted most of the power to remain with the state governments. The first plan for the national government was called the **Articles of Confederation.** Congress accepted this plan in 1777.

The United States had many problems under the Articles. The government needed money, but only the states could collect taxes. The states often refused to give tax money to the national government. The states acted like separate countries.

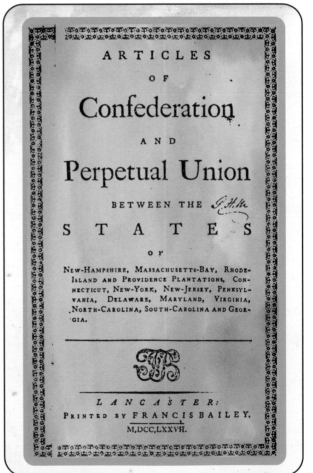

▶ *The Articles of Confederation*

The U.S. Constitution

In 1787, state representatives met again to write a new plan for the national government. The meeting was called the Constitutional **Convention**. The leaders chose George Washington to be president of the meeting. The new government plan was called the United States Constitution. The Constitution gave more power to the national government and less to the states.

▼ *The United States Constitution was signed by Congress on September 17, 1787.*

The Constitution

The Constitution explains that there are three branches of government. The legislative branch makes the laws. It includes two **houses** of Congress: The House of Representatives and the Senate. The executive branch is led by the president and ensures that the laws are carried out. The judicial branch is made of courts and judges. They interpret, or explain, the laws.

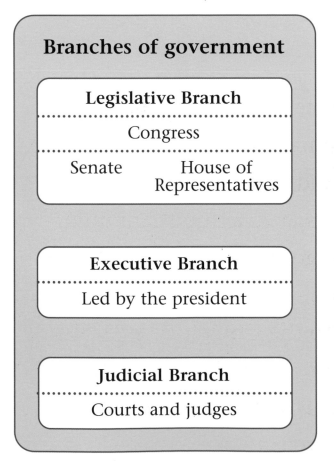

Branches of government

Legislative Branch

Congress

Senate   House of Representatives

Executive Branch

Led by the president

Judicial Branch

Courts and judges

▲ *James Madison wrote many parts of the Constitution.*

Lessons from history

Some of James Madison's ideas for the Constitution came from Britain's Magna Carta. In 1215, people in Britain gathered together and forced their king, John, to sign this document. The Magna Carta took some powers from the king and gave them to the people.

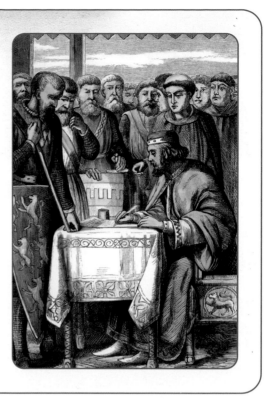

▶ *King John signing the Magna Carta*

For or against?

After the Constitution was written, the states had to approve it. Americans who wanted the Constitution were called Federalists. Those who did not want it were called Anti-Federalists. Anti-Federalists were afraid that, under the Constitution, the national government would be too powerful and would take rights away from people. In the end, all 13 states voted "yes" to the Constitution. Many of them asked for something in return, however. They wanted to add a Bill of Rights. This addition would protect the people from the government.

The First Amendment

The Bill of Rights was added to the Constitution on December 15, 1791. It consists of the first ten amendments to the Constitution. The Bill of Rights lists freedoms that all Americans have. It says that the government cannot stop Americans from enjoying these freedoms unless the government has a very good reason.

◄ George Washington was made the first U.S. president in 1789. A new president must promise to "preserve, protect, and defend the Constitution of the United States."

Freedom of speech

The leaders who wrote the Bill of Rights remembered that British soldiers had arrested people who spoke against King George III. They remembered how the king had made the colonists stop having meetings. The First Amendment ensured that this would never happen again in the United States. This amendment says that Americans can share their beliefs, no matter what those beliefs are. Americans can have meetings, give speeches, carry signs, write stories, and sing songs about anything they want.

▼ *Americans can speak freely, even if other people disagree.*

Freedom of the Press

In 1734, New York was a colony. John Peter Zenger was a local newspaper printer in the colony. Some of his stories criticized the colony's British **governor.** The stories said that the governor was unfair to colonists. The governor arrested Zenger and sent him to jail to stop the criticisms.

The next year, John Peter Zenger went on trial so that a jury of citizens could decide if he deserved to be in jail. The jury, guided by a judge, decided that Zenger should be freed. They felt he was allowed to print whatever he wanted as long as it was true.

▶ *Colonists read reports and stories printed in newspapers. The newspapers were sold in shops.*

▲ *John Peter Zenger was tried in a court before a judge and jury.*

Reporting the news

When it was time to write the Bill of Rights, Americans remembered this trial and wanted to add freedom of the press as an amendment. The "press" now includes anything that people use to report the news, such as radio, TV, newspapers, and the Internet. In many countries, the government stops the news from being reported. The Bill of Rights does not allow this in the United States.

Freedom of Religion

The First Amendment of the Bill of Rights also promises freedom of religion. This allows Americans to believe and worship in any religion, or none at all. Also, the United States government cannot support any one religion. In 1776, Britain supported a religion called the Church of England. The King of England was the head of the church. People who did not belong to this religion could lose their jobs or homes, or be put in jail.

▲ *Jewish people built this synagogue in Newport, Rhode Island, in 1763. It was the first synagogue in the United States.*

It shall not happen again

Many people moved to America because they wanted freedom of religion. They did not have this in Britain. However, in the early days of the colonies, some people were punished for their religious beliefs. Freedom of religion was added to the Bill of Rights to stop such things from happening.

The trial
In 1637, a woman named Anne Hutchinson was leader of the Puritan religion in Massachusetts. Some of her beliefs were different from the other Puritans. Massachusetts leaders forced Anne Hutchison out of the colony because of her different beliefs.

Live and Let Live

The Second Amendment says that people have the right *"to keep and bear arms."* This means that citizens who behave well can keep guns at home to protect themselves. During the American Revolution, Patriots had wanted to protect themselves from British soldiers. They had also wanted to be able to protect themselves from their national leaders if these people became unfair.

◄ *Patriot soldiers used guns to fight the British.*

Privacy

The Third Amendment of the Bill of Rights ensures that the government cannot force people to allow soldiers to live in their houses, as the British had done to the colonists. The Fourth Amendment gives Americans rights to privacy. For example, the police may not search a person's property unless there is a good reason to believe the person has committed a crime. The police must prove to a judge why the search should take place.

▲ *A police officer can ask to search a person's car if he or she thinks there might be stolen property in the vehicle.*

Limiting Power

The first eight amendments of the Bill of Rights list the rights that Americans will always have. The Ninth Amendment says that the national government cannot take away other rights, even if those rights are not named in the Constitution. For example, people have the right to travel freely between the states. The Tenth Amendment stops the national government from taking on more powers than those that are listed in the Constitution.

▼ *You can see the Declaration of Independence, the Constitution, and the Bill of Rights in the National Archives in Washington, D.C.*

Seeking justice

Sometimes, people think their rights have been violated. For example, people may say they have been denied freedom of speech. These people go to court to ask a judge or jury to decide if their treatment goes against the Bill of Rights. If people do not agree with a court's decision, they may take it to a higher court. The Supreme Court, the nation's highest court, has made many decisions about whether or not the Bill of Rights has been upheld.

▼ *The nine justices (judges) of the Supreme Court meet in this building.*

Still Growing

The first ten amendments were an important addition to the Constitution. Other amendments were added over the years. The Constitution has rules for adding amendments. First, both houses of Congress must pass the amendment. Then three-fourths of the states must approve it. So far, more than 9,000 amendments have been proposed to Congress but only 27 have been added to the Constitution.

▼ *Members of the Senate vote on new amendments to the Bill of Rights.*

▲ *Before the Nineteenth Amendment was passed, women marched in Washington, D.C., demanding their right to vote.*

A lasting document

Some new amendments caused important changes in the United States. In 1865, the Thirteenth Amendment ended slavery. People could no longer own slaves. A slave is a person who works hard for no pay. In 1920, the Nineteenth Amendment gave women the right to vote.

Since the Constitution was signed, the nation has grown from 13 to 50 states. For more than 200 years, the Constitution has guided the United States government, and the Bill of Rights has protected its citizens.

Timeline

1637 Anne Hutchinson is forced out of Massachusetts because of her religious beliefs

1735 John Peter Zenger goes on trial for criticizing the British governor in a local newspaper

1760s Britain passes new taxes for colonists

1774 The First Continental Congress meets to discuss how to deal with Britain's taxes and rules

1775 First shots of the American Revolution are fired

1776 The Continental Congress signs the Declaration of Independence

1777 The Articles of Confederation become the first plan of national government

1781 Americans win the American Revolution

1783 A peace treaty ends the American Revolution

1787 Representatives meet at the Constitutional Convention to revise the Articles of Confederation. Instead, a new U.S. Constitution is written

1788 The Constitution becomes official after nine states accept it

1791 The Bill of Rights becomes part of the Constitution

Websites

1. Ben's Guide to U.S. Government for Kids
http://bensguide.gpo.gov/3-5/citizenship/rights.html
On this site you will find information about the Bill of Rights, and about
becoming an American citizen and the responsibilities of American citizens.

2. The White House for Kids
http://www.whitehouse.gov/kids/constitution/billofrights.html
Here you will find a list of each amendment in the Bill of Rights,
with a link to Constitutional amendments 11–27.

3. National Archives and Records Administration
http://www.archives.gov/exhibits/charters/bill_of_rights.html
This site includes a transcript of the Bill of Rights, an image of
the original document, and links to other sites of interest.

4. The Constitution for Kids
http://www.usconstitution.net/constkids.html
Look at this site for background information on the Constitution and a link to
the Bill of Rights topic page (http://www.usconstitution.net/consttop_bor.html).

5. Congress for Kids
http://www.congressforkids.net/Independence_articles.htm
Go to this website for history of the Articles of Confederation, plus a multiple-choice
quiz, and links to other fun quizzes about the Articles and the Constitution.

Further Reading

Burgan, Michael. *The Bill of Rights*. Mankato, Minn.: Compass Point, 2002.
Hamilton, John. *The Bill of Rights*. Edina, Minn: ABDO, 2004.
Krull, Kathleen. A *Kid's Guide to America's Bill of Rights*. New York: Avon, 1999.
Rivera, Sheila. *The Bill of Rights*. Edina, Minn: ABDO, 2004.
Stein, R. Conrad. *The Bill of Rights*. Children's Press, 1992.
Taylor-Butler, Christine. *The Bill of Rights*. New York: Scholastic, 2008.
Teitelbaum, Michael. *The Bill of Rights*. Mankato, Minn.: Child's World, 2004.
Yero, Judith Lloyd. *American Documents: The Bill of Rights*. Washington, D.C.: National
     Geographic, 2006.

Glossary

amendment An addition or change

American Revolution The war of independence from Britain

Articles of Confederation An early plan for the national government

Bill of Rights Additions to the U.S. Constitution

colony A place where people live that is far from the country that rules it

Constitution A written plan or set of rules for the United States government

Continental Congress A meeting of representatives to discuss a subject; Congress is also the group of lawmakers in the United States

convention A meeting of representatives

Declaration of Independence A document claiming the right of Americans to make their own decisions and laws

government The group of people who run the country or state

governor The person in charge of a colony or state

house A part or division of Congress

jury A group of people at a trial who decide if a person is guilty or not

Patriot A person who fought for independence from Britain

representative Someone who speaks for many people

revolution A strong action by people to change their government

tax Money paid by people to the government to run the country

trial An event in court that presents information so that a judge or jury can decide if someone committed a crime

Index

32

Printed in the U.S.A. – BG